Twilight Murders, other Poems and Essays

Kuir ë Garang

TNP

The Nile Press
Calgary, Alberta

First Edition 2016

ISBN: 978-0-9938279-2-1

PUBLISHED BY THE NILE PRESS
http://www.thenilepress.com
Calgary
Printed in USA

Kuir ë Garang is a South Sudanese poet, writer and author currently living in Calgary, Alberta. For more information about the author and all his writings, visit his website at www.kuirthiy.com.

Other titles by the author

1. South Sudan Ideologically (2013)
2. Is 'Black' Really Beautiful? (2013)
3. The Carcass Valley (2016)
4. The Pipers and the First Phase (2012)
5. Exegesis of Despotism (2011)
6. Deng, Nyan-Nhialdit and the Talking Crow

"Sometimes I think that a parody of democracy could be more dangerous than a blatant dictatorship, because that gives people an opportunity to avoid doing anything about it."

~ Aung San Suu Kyi

Diing Chan Awuol (Isaiah Abraham) –
Photo Courtesy of Awak Deng Bior

For Isaiah Abraham and all the South Sudanese martyrs

TABLE OF CONTENTS

Poetry is sometimes considered (or denigrated) as an emotive fancy or a mental demystification of the monotonousness of life and known realities. True! It takes *the poet* (and the reader following later) to the fantastical (or ideal) world many just imagine but wait for the poet to expose. This *nonscientific*, metaphysical or emotive demystification is in fact an unconscious defiance towards the *known*, the *mundane*...the relevant collectivities in life 'that are just always there.' This defiance against the boring, oppressive *reality* of existence is akin to the oppressive reality different minorities face; and the defiance they feel against established sociocultural institutions, which intentionally or inadvertently exclude them.

With this defiance against existential reality in mind, we can conceptualize that narrative conflicts aren't exclusively fictional or literary realities, nor are they literal, practical realities we face as we forage through life's complexities in our everyday living! Mere Existence *itself* can be a formidable conflict. *Existence* conflicts are existential and ontological realities. We can never exist as *beings* in a 'conflict' free existence. Existence in-itself is conflictual. We live in a Marxian cosmos whether in the classical, economic, Marxist sense, or in a more modified social, Williamian sense (William, 1991).

Undoubtedly, we are always 'against something': material or spiritual, or ghostly. Our triumph in this existential and ontological conflict determines our general mood or place in life: happy or defeated, conquered or triumphant, rich or poor.... Albert Camus ([1955] 1983)) *absurdity* captures this existential reality with a flamboyant genius: suicide or life (bad as it is).

So, this conflict, between various internalized conceptualization of *the self*, between external rationalization of one's self and external rationalization of one self by others, and between one's social position and one's response to it, is the lived reality of the African Person: spiritually and materially. It's a grand fight, but the African Person wants to fight (or resist) in a manner that'd be deemed 'respectable' to the opposing side in this socio-intellectual conflict. Critical Theory, among others, is one tool in this conflict. Poetry in this collection, is another tool.

Critical Theory (CT) while very much despised—for obvious reasons—by established cultural orthodoxy or conservativism, has a lot to teach us in terms of the humanity and humility of any given, dominant societal consciousness. And this is very important when we discursively study 'what is already there' and subjecting it to rigorous scrutiny in order to ascertain its inclusiveness and importance in terms of the values required by contemporary realities.

This 'scrutiny' doesn't always come unchallenged nor is it always a welcome 'change.' Cultural Theorists used CT to make society more culturally inclusive by adopting a self-righteous and more antagonistic, corrective way of 'changing' society. Without doubt, such oppositional and resistance-based (Sieler, 2015) ways of making societies more inclusive are very tempting. And indeed, the collection of poems in this book can't help but follow the same line of defiance in the face of what has already been established as the naturalized (Giroux et al, 2015) reality. However, there are two ways of going about this: One way is to resist these objectified subjectivities with an aim to change them and change the society; however, another way is to put out a resisting consciousness whether or not it will change anything in the society (Williams, 1991).

The collection of poems and three reflective essays aim at presenting a poetic resistance to unacceptable state of affairs. It follows the latter form of 'resistance' if this poetic presentation qualifies at all as 'resistance.' The reality defied here is spiritual, material, mentally external and internal, national and international, patriarchal, racial, political, social, religious, and filial.

Reading this poetry book would therefore be readers' cordial entry into a fantastical (if critical) African mind, into a subaltern mind, into a mind affected by war and societal judgements; a mind that wants to make people talk or mentally agitated …a mind that doesn't simply want to change societal consciousness.

Kuir ë Garang
Calgary, Alberta
October 12, 2015

Citations

Camus, A. ([1955] 1991). *The Myth of Sisyphus and Other Essays*. New York: Vintage International

Giroux, H. et al. (2015). *The Need for Cultural Studies: Resisting Intellectuals and Oppositional Public Spheres*.
Retrieved (September 26)
(http://theory.eserver.org/need.html)

Seiler, R. M. (2015). *Human Communication in the British Cultural Studies Tradition*. Retrieved on September 26.
(http://people.ucalgary.ca/~rseiler/british.htm).

Williams, R. (1991). "Base and Superstructure in Marxist Cultural Theory." In. *Rethinking Popular Culture*. Chandra Mukerji and Michael Schudson, .Ed. Los Angeles: University of California Press.

The Philosophical 'Refugee': Obscure Mind, Obscure Humanity, Obscure Thoughts!

"No one leaves home unless home
is the mouth of a shark."

— Warsan Shire

IMAGINE BEING born in a country in which you're consid-
ered a 'slave' — in the 21st century — because of *who* you are. Imagine
living in a country where your true humanity, true history, true *sense of
self,* is someone else's inconvenience. And imagine being on a constant
move – in search of safety – as a child, a refugee whose prospects of expe-
riencing what it means to be a *person* (a social subject, a political agent)
with a state, a citizenship, exist only as a dream, a 'beautiful' dream whose
possibility of fulfilment is itself a stress simply because of its realization
impossibility.

And imagine a chillingly debilitating possibility of one being a refugee
for eternity; of living with the feeling that you'll always be a 'refugee' and

perpetually stateless. And imagine someone oppressing you because of the erroneous, interpretive biblical assumptions that you're divinely punished; and the horror unleashed upon you is a godly pronouncement.

You'd think this isn't pretty, or it's even sad! And sadly, this has been some people's true state of affairs; a condition in life that, unfortunately, some people still live in.

And imagine being assumed unintelligent all the time until you open your mouth; being considered dangerous and violent until you smile to assure anyone present that you're a peaceful mind and heart. And imagine being treated with a flattering condescension and paternalism because you look a certain way.

For a war-child, living as a refugee and moving to a land where your look, and your look alone, is your humanity, is a great disservice to one's *sense of self*.

However, what's comforting for me is that the above disconcerting and seemingly fictitious human conditions have only done a lot to straighten my thoughts about humanity. They've made me a person whose brain is made up of nothing but thoughts, lots of thoughts…eye opening army of thoughts (*thoughtons* if you like).

However, these thoughts are always in a constant belligerence with societal assumptions about me, the African Person. Of course, the assumptions are imposed with historical and empirical support, and this makes the assumptions powerfully affecting. I have to defy these societal assumptions about the African Person. But what power do I have as an African Person in Canada, in the world? How can I shake off caricatures that have been in the making and enforcement for hundreds of years? Who'd listen to me even when I shout social MAYDAYS? Perhaps overt defiance itself is naive and proves *their* point!

My silence is my natural state, supposedly. My actional, human errors are my nature. Indeed, my nature is what I do, not something separable from myself *per se*. So, who'd listen to me? Who'd dare give me a chance?

Perhaps I'm supposed to be heeded only when I feel sorry for myself; when I present myself as a helpless, despondent refugee! Only then does the world find a heart-warming story; the pious unleashes his godliness, and the capitalist becomes a philanthropist. Sadly, that is the required me. But no, I'll not do that, and I'll not be that fellow, the fellow swimming in required, infinite haplessness. I'll defy but still respect the world.

I have (and will indeed continue to) put all these inconveniencing pollywogs (thoughts) twirling in my head to work in a manner both required and not required.

However, my thoughts are considered obscure, nonsensical, and incomprehensible. But then I smile, heartily! Their incomprehensibility is the very nature of their beauty, their therapeutic essence. Their helpfulness is one's struggle to understand them. And I choose to be obscure! And this chosen obscurity has made me impervious to assumptions, inconsiderate assumptions about who I am, where I am from and what I do.

I've lived long enough in Canada to be a Canadian citizen; however, I'm still at the periphery of what makes the soul of Canada. I'm still a refugee, a curiosity inviting person. My Canadian passport is just but a paper to Canada. It's a mark of citizenship, of belonging to the beauty Canada is. But no, Canada doesn't think so. I'm still a refugee, an illiterate, violent, hopeless refugee. Still, I defy this status quo because someone inside me still believes there is someone in this society that will still believe me; someone who'd think my thoughts are not obscure, that they just need a humble study. She's humbled herself down to a point of naivety to understand why I look the way I look; why I talk the way I talk; and why I don't follow the best, the smartest and the industrious. Maybe I'm not obscure, incomprehensible for nothing!

But why can't I, like other *words'* people, be explicit and simply understood. I don't know. I don't even know who I am. But perhaps I'm just lying.

I pour words into paper like water into a glass, a shiny crystal-clear glass. I release thoughts and then twist them so intricately that their receivers are left scratching their heads as to what I meant. I rap my poetry so softly that listeners wonder. I write beautiful poetry, as Liz said, but I'm still obscure. I theorize with unorthodox edge that my readers stare with puzzling awe, thinking: "Who is this?"

Who am I? Am I a rapper, or a poet, a novelist, a burgeoning publisher or just a 'refugee'? Am I just a written off wanderer in a beautiful country, or a voice of the refugee child, a war-child? Am I just being antithetical to beautiful thoughts?

The more I write the more I feel fresh, alive and confident; and the more I become incomprehensible and obscure. My dark face and dark skin symbolize the condition with metaphysical dimension.

Perhaps, I should rap my poetry and stop putting it into print. But no, I can't do that. I want to be confident, to be alive, to be mentally healthy.

Who am I? I'm the waster of your time, the obscurity to be unravelled, the hidden pearl only valued by the 'unraveller' of the obscure.

DIVINE OR DIVINIZED MISOGYNY, AND THE CALLOUS ME

Part One: Divine or Divinized Misogyny

For all the beautiful hearts broken

It's Sunday morning and I'm ready for a lot
I love the gospel music sound: message not!
Don't get me wrong. I've read the wise men
Get me wrong here for, they, enslaved women:
(Genesis 19: 7-8; 31-36, Judges 19: 25-27)
Three gods and they are all, mysteriously, one [He] man
Within the gentlemen's circle, not a single woman
The Son of Joseph assumed god's fatherhood
Well, we wish god's fatherhood in our neighborhoods
The son of Joseph loved women
But the wise men treated women like omen
In the Trinity the third one should have been a female
That fairness could've absolved the wise males
One male, one female, the third a hermaphrodite
That Trinity could've given women so much pride
It's fairness the wise men couldn't stomach
Is it fear or hate of the woman? She's given us so much
Son of Joseph had some in company
The wise men only acknowledged 12 men in harmony
That thought alone makes San Franciscans (SFs) smile
So much is said now by the wise to make SFs senile
But does the son of Joseph love the giver of life?
I don't know for his father didn't like them either
I can say that and in it be firmer
Periods reign hell on her with excruciating pain
Labor screams make one doubt god, time and again
The male makes a face of a pained carer

20

The schmuck is only a sympathetic starer
Maybe the wise men are not to blame
Their god's nature and work mirror the insane
Biblical misogyny is too hard to ignore
After birth she stays up only for him to snore
I don't know the misogynist: god or the fellows
I'm sorry but I'm no longer mellow
There used to be goddesses and priestesses
The wise mocks the idea of the female priest
When was the woman ever valued?
She sinned in the garden: bad values
She had a virgin birth: innocence
Virginity boosts men egos not girls' prominence
So don't mention that mocking essence!
I say this not that I don't care
Well, I accept being insouciant
Yours sincerely, the broken fellow!

Part Two: The Callous Me

The Wonky Fellow

Why's the woman always in pain?
Because she doesn't pretend to be insane
I hide my pain and smile a way the sorrow
Then poor me is tormented every tomorrow
It's not that I'm not in painful thought
I've been broken time again, so I just rot
I've seen your tears drop
I've heard your cries but didn't say stop
I know it sounds callous;
Heartlessness that could be disastrous
I'm a glass with a crack you can't see

I could've been gentlemanly and let you be
But now I feel what is true
It's the fear of a broken soul to break through
So now I'm the victim when she's the one
Call me heartless, I deserve it like none
I have a sharp brain so don't get me wrong
You can brand me a trite wonk
But I have a heart only a few can afford to have
I don't know why it makes you underserved
Maybe I'm just irreparable and reserved
The O'sun rises and you yearn for that softest touch
So, do the nostalgic memories to dream as such
Call me a beautiful heart that'll never be
Call me a sweet face you'll never see
You're the heart desired to the end
You've been, among other things, a good friend
I've become a banal fellow seen smiling
But I'm a desensitized heart that keeps struggling
I'd love you to understand for you're beautiful and kind
I'd love you to have good things, not by design
I've been paralyzed so I know how those shoes feel
Too many hearts I've broken
That's the problem for the beautiful heart that's shaken
I know it makes no sense at all
But you'll grace the floor in deserving hand in your ball
It's not that I don't care
It's just that I've been too desensitized, to be fair
You can see men are always in pain indeed
Only that you can't see
I say this not that I don't care
Well, I accept being insouciant
Yours sincerely, the broken fellow!

THE STRENGTH WITHIN YOU (PART I)

(For our mother, AJah Garang Manyang)

In you we have the greatest hope
In you lies the genial of all hearts
In you we have what we need to be
In you we'll strive to always be good…
You, the amazing mother!

In you we have the strength to cope
In you we smile when things get hard
In you is the world we've come to see
In you, ideas become our daily food…
You, the amazing mother!

With you, life becomes a gentle slope
With you, difficulty is only a good start
With you dad lives on for us to be
In you is a mother that makes us good…
Thank you…the amazing mother!

FOR YOU SOUTH SUDAN STANDS STRONG! (PART II)

(For every South Sudanese mother)

You've filled the Nile with blood
You've teared full the land like flood
Your hungry child cries, you helpless
No tears left as you stare breathless
But your steely heart is full of grits
I know you're not a happy mother now
But the strength you exude makes us bow

We're full of bitterness and loss so heavy
But your forgiving heart is peace privy
And for you, the South stands strong!
Mother's Day but you're not in Bor
Mother's Day and Bentiu is burnt-down stores
Mother's Day and Malakal is a ghost town
In the Equatorias the guns still sound
But you advise us to clean our hearts of hate
As you stand scotched by the merciless heat
Snakes, scorpions, birds have things to eat
And that's you and your kids
You walked for months but stronger
You've lost everything but still prouder
Amazing you still remain the amazing mother
Resilient and loving like no any other
In UNMISS dungeons you still cry peace
A beautiful heart we should have in deeds
They ignore you under a shadow-less tree
You still smile with open heart even not pleased
That's hope we need when all is sorrow
On Mother's Day you're our tomorrow
Day and night, you're the rational voice
The silent suffering should be the loud noise
As hatred floats and flies over the land
Resilience and hope is your safest hand
You've lost so much and that's so wrong
But still, you make the South stand strong!
It isn't a happy day, but it's your day
The day of the strongest *woman on earth!*
The day for the one above all, *the best!*
I salute you…you, the Southern Mother!

MADIBA, YOU CAN GO NOW!

(Tribute to Mandela)

Remarkable! You not only existed, you truly lived
Blessed generations to be endowed with peaceful deeds
True greatness is never lost across all times
Through the rough of it all, the peace bell still chimes
We walk every day in the shadows of oppression
Weakness of heart you tied down in a joyous suppression
They called you Rolihlahla in tribal symbolism
And what a good trouble you brought us in true nationalism
You troubled the trouble to breed precise humility
You broke the back of oppression with crystal simplicity
Our heavy hearts rewind to your remarkable African-*ness*
All the dark faces have been shown the truest kindness
It's remarkable the inspiration wasn't foreign
You twinned the mind and heart in a consistent run
We could have picked up guns and spears
But, you, Madiba emerged to simplify our fears
We've always been trampled upon for so much a time
We've absorbed immorality and divine crime
But that darkness and hatred is what you'd later despise
27 you weathered so simply with no hate inside
Who knew hatred is weakness presented as spite?
You've shown that spite and hatred are a weakness' desire
Who now talks fondly of your jailors except the stinky mire
Values and virtues the true height and driver of civilizations
If only they become the light for every nation

You've shown with remarkable fervor their validity
The *African Self* is a box full of values quiddity
The ingenious tradition and African-*ness* unmatched
Generations will smile-in Madiba's life from scratch
Forgiveness always is what you've forever sown
Humility in deeds is what we've come to know
Race is only a concept if not an intellectual quest
Madiba, you're gone but we're left with a clean path, I guess
Why should we cry when your humility is here?
Why would we mourn when your deeds we hear?
We've not built rockets and cars
But Mandela has been ours
You can go now, Madiba!
The life you lived is the way the world should be!

TRITE WONK

There's this counselor I don't want to know
Because I have tears I don't want to show
For years I've had a very pained heart
I guess it's a result of goodness from the start
But who'll know the pain of tears not shed?
Who'll know death inside, gloom so sad?
For the world a sad man is a crying man
But the silent is suicidal and on the sand…
Or the suited, happy fellow in a leather chair…
I didn't know the truth helps the noisy ones
Who'd want to wait to verify? I guess none!
The trite wonk is very quiet but still loud
The trite wonk is very humble but proud
The trite wonk says the truth but hypocritical
The trite wonk is ideal but practical
He's traveled a road few have used
His silence is the drug being abused
What's life if silence is the mood?
What's life if respect becomes crude?
Respect makes him the weakest link
But he'd pledged to keep his word and never think
The trite wonk's face is a sad countenance
But his inner man smiles are his ordinance
Silence & Respect are his badge
From now on the TW takes the pledge
I AM …THE TRITE WONK!

TRUTH AT ALL COST

(*Tribute to Uncle Elijah Malok Aleng*)

We'll not cry tears now for you left a legacy
Your words and ideals were loud to fight a fallacy
Valuing truth all the time was your defining feature
Even when Pundits felt it caused unnerving fissures
You left for liberation at your youthful prime
Because being an African was indeed a crime
But never did you buy into that medieval fuss
You walked foreign bushes and capitals for us,
For generations that'd be born into oppression
Oduho, Saturnino and Jaden wanted separation
Separation of truth from fallacy for the African Child
But it'd be many years of blood and tears in the wild
But valor was in you glistening and beaming
Oduho valued your youth & wisdom from the beginning
John Garang would later second the truth you say
It wasn't always easy to be you from day to day
But you valued truth as your characterizing pillar
Youngsters will ask themselves how to be similar
Truth is a dangerous, hot metal few dare hold, face
In the labyrinth of liberation fire and race,
Truth is sacrificed for opportunity and fear
The burden of truth is one thing you came to bear
You rejected being nice if it compromised valued norms
How many men would pride in that enviable form?
You coupled a fierce tongue with a valued simplicity
You never sought power with your valued utility
You went to the bush *twice* with historical giants
And you remained in the bush with a patriotic compliance

28

South Sudan says, 'thank you!' for yo' time and knowledge
Jonglei State has in you a historical son to acknowledge
The Twi Child adds you to the long list of valued men gone
Wangulei will have one thing for generations not yet born
When the storm is over, Awulian will smile;
Smile for the ideal you inculcated not just for a while
The Twi Child will tell the South Sudanese...
Truth at all Cost, all the time, please!
Now, it's time to say "Bye" and "Rest in Peace Uncle Elijah!"

THE DREAM OF TWÏ CHILD

Out of the shadows of paralysis you'll rise
Oh, South Sudan, abused you've been!
So much emotions and misery you've seen!
I'll stand on the canal to make all awed
Development will be a song than a thought
Years of destructive indifference will be surmised;
Surmised into twilight hope for all to be surprised,
Out of ruins, like smoke, you will rise
Like genies out of bottles, schools will sprout
Perhaps I'm just a dreamer, but I'm proud
A proud Twï Child with a purpose
I'll turn the flooded plains into lash terrains;
The Twï Child will tell South Sudan, 'brains!'
'Use your brains to wipe the Southern child's tears'
"Use your hearts to rid mothers of natal fears'
Ah, I know the heart of the Twi denizens
From warriors to development citizens
Need I not worry!
The determined remnants of war are out
They'd drunk directly from infested rivers
And they were destroyed by dangerous fevers
It's now time to drink clean waters
But who'll make it possible for us?
Whose hands are so generous?
Little girls in *Maar* yearn for equipped clinics
Young boys in *Paliau* don't want to be cynics
Will that new born in *Wangulei* reach five?
How about that expectant mother with her cows?
She wants to stroll majestically to *Pawel*
Who'll tarmac her bike path to *Panyagoor*?
And just think of that old man sitting under the tree

He's diabetic and needs his wheelchair to be free
I, the Twï Child, will help grandma smile
Who'll join me to *Wernyol*. . .just for a few miles?
Oh, I know, we'll make South Sudan rise
And out of 'Twic East County' It'll rise
Development is the song I'll sing!
Let the Twï Child grow up worry free!
And that's the Twi Child's dream, you see?

I WISHED I COULD JUST BE

~ Inside the poet's mind ~

I wished I was a bird to fly
I wished I was water to evaporate, not appear
I wished I was a morning dew to disappear
I wished I was air to gently flow by
I wish I could just be…

I wished I could not hear any song
I wished I could not see any throng
I wished I could not taste something sweet
I wished I could not smell my own sweat
I wish I could just be…

I wished I had no legs to walk around
I wished I had no mouth to utter a sound
I wished I had no heart that cares
I wished I was just a child to just stare
I wish I could just be…

I wished I was just an imbecile
I wished I was never but still
I wished I was nowhere but here
I wished I was nonexistent but there
I wish I could just be…

I wished I was that valueless being
I wished I was a cow on the slaughter line
I wished I was the lion's prey, never seeing
I wished I was just blind
I wish I could just be…

I wished there was no knife on my neck
I wished no obstruction for my breath
I wished there was no smile, my last step
I wished I was here on this earth
I wish I could just be…

I wished on earth there was smile
I wished on earth there was mine
I wished on earth there was life
I wished on earth there wasn't crime
I just wish I could just be…

I wished I was a bird to fly
I wished I was water to evaporate, not appear
I wished I was a morning dew to disappear
I wished I was air to gently flow by
I wished you were here
I wished I was there…
I wish I could just be…

WHY ARE WE NOT RIDICULOUS?

Ravi calls death our greatest enemy
But it's the only thing through
Which we're equal.
For death our destination is one
Death is certainty for humanity
For death there's no racial exception
For death there's no size or strength
For death there's no poor or rich
For death there's no choice of an escape
For death there's no last laugh
Hawkings talks of blackholes
Science struggles at CERN
But here's one giant blackhole
Who'd escape it?
My only egalitarian friend: Death!
...
We call love the best thing
But for it we are all restless
For love we're jealous
For love we scheme
For love friendships unravel
For love we lose ourselves...
Love is temporary
Love isn't even certain
Yet we glorify love...
For love we divide humanity
In and for love we prefer
For love egalitarianism is fallacious
...
When do we say the truth?
When we aren't ridiculous!

And that's when we cease!
For love you're less to a person
For death, you'll all be the same
How are we not ridiculous?
You can ask Thatcher if you can!

IT'S OKAY SON [RESPECT!]

We've dodged them same bullets
It's not the time to pull it
Heaviness in heart we share
It seems the same...you don't care
The crescent scar on my feet
Frowns at me so innocent in deeds
But it's okay son! Respect!

Civility is earned I shoulda known
Stop looking up we're all blown
One thing I rejected from dad
Intrepid then but now I see that
We've all been schooled, we discern (ed)
Innocent you are...I am concerned
But it's ok son! Respect!

Felonious writs aren't me
Unlike the ciphers you'll see
Scholastic you've forgotten
You've concealed a little to soften
Respect for *the man* under every tree
South has a lot of mangoes for us to be free
But it's ok son! Respect!

SOUTH SUDAN, I CRY FOR YOU!

When we become imbeciles

In living memory, you were well guarded
In wild bushes roamed true heroes well regarded
Innumerable fools now and you're discarded
Freedom finished us to be relatively free
Freedom fighters now continue to decrease
Across the river is a bunch of power douche
A long the flanks of the Nile: ecstasy and booze
Freedom is now my fictitious invention
The near fellow has authenticated my assumption
South Sudan, I cry for you!

Ministers with brains full of maggots!
Tomfoolery across the board if you forgot
The old farts are all brain dead
The naïve young can't define the nation's fate
Tribe and power the deathly combination
Luxurious education the young observation
They passed through and back with new bargain
Hatred they breathe but deny it all the same
South Sudan, I cry for you!

Tribes are dying under the orange Sun
Self-righteous tribes believed the only sons
Death on the streets but the educated celebrate
Stupidity ubiquitous and indeterminate

37

Only a few I've seen truly mourning
A pained heart, no hate ...come what morning!
Future leaders are fools in educated skin
Tribism celebrated in rejecting tribalism
I'm so sad in this douche bags' prism
South Sudan, I cry for you!

Imbecility is all I see around
After sanity who'll be held to account
Respect will become a commodity
How would I dispense it? Such an oddity!
Filthy mouths can't even make us breathe
Dodos' thoughts, words flying. . .just read!
Yesterday like today, filled with mediocrity
Tomorrow the death of alacrity
South Sudan, I cry for you!

DEAR WAU, YOU ARE ALONE!

Tribute!

We called them freedom fighters
They were young and determined
They left schools, jobs, cattle camps…
It was a time for the land defenders;
To portray the same inner strength
The Arab enslavers admired in them…
Now the strength was to dispel sickly piety,
They didn't know all gods are the same
But as they trekked to *Bonga* and *Bilpam,*
Their learned leaders showed another world;
A world in which they had a voice!
Beautiful it was…more determined
They became…prouder as they laughed,
But oblivious they were of the journey,
It was only six months and the
Enemy would go back to Gezira!
That clever man had some nerves,
It would be over twenty years of
Bloodiness and grueling politicking…
But the dear doctor had a mind, heart
He felt sorry for the freedom fighters:
Barefoot, hungry, naked, drenched
In blood, rain and flood…
It had to end…the doctor smiled!
Then nature called before *he* prepared
The table for the meal for us all,
Our nation's sky was humidified by
Our tears and sad, running noses,
Our wailing and cries shook the

Savannah and the Rain Forest…
He was gone, perhaps he was taken…
But we were consoled…by whom?
The leftovers of the twenty years
Of bloodiness…yes…
They were freedom fighters then…
I don't know what happened
After the doctor slept so soon…
They sit on big comforts and shoot at us!
Dear Wau, I don't know what happened!
Maybe they consume a lot now…
Rapacious, scared and Benjamin-crazy!
They *eat* our dollars, *drink* our oil
And *butcher* our opinion writers…
And then they *mow* you down…
Dear Wau, we're soul-searching!
Our gods were killed by Christians,
Who thought that we were slaves by divine
Design, so take heart…you're alone,
We are all asking what happened to them.
Where are the freedom fighters?
Why are we seeing only villains?
Why are we seeing only carnivores?
What happened to freedom fighters?
Oh dear Wau: 1965, 1998, 2012?

THE TWILIGHT MURDERS

Villagers squirmed, guns multiplied, that momentous rumble
We'd transiently bottled our fears before siblings assembled
The *clarion call* was heeded with grits of an awakened soul
It'd be May like no any other two decades after the first call,

It was time when *honor* meant impeccable brotherhood
It was time when good deeds were respected along the Sudd
The then quiescent spirits married greed to flex away feeble minds
The rapacious weaklings redefined the liberation designs,

The orange sun's tongue would kiss the horizontal lips
However, the romantic imagination was marred like a blip
Hope became an itsy bitsy blip as brotherhood fanned out
Fanned out as fellowship dwindled into an egregious shout-out,

Young Akuol, who'd craved freedom, stared in dreadful awe
The bayonet was now working left and right like a saw
Sisters and brothers murdered honor at sundown
The Western brothers used it to claim honors at Sundance,

Educated fools and educated foxes sneaked through the *smoke*
Young Nyachiengkuoth waited for words but no one spoke
Knowledge and literary excellence meant death back home
Soldiers limped back home with wounds after the storm,

Ojullu and Nyoka rested on the Nile Bank in consternation
They'd hoped the crazy liberators would think of a nation
Policy papers became double-edged weapons along the way
Respect was buried in the training camp, honor flexed away,

The docs worshipped narcissism, so I hoped the young would learn

41

Honor was sliced sunrise to sunset to polished minds in turns
The enemy was redefined for survival, so it became the norm
Conscience sickened as the south swam in *bloods* and bones,

Twenty years later, respect and honor are all dead and buried
Jealousy is worshipped with an artistic semblance and varied
Juba celebrates murderous adventures to stifle prosperity
The young buying into the culture with foolish severity,

The 'liberators' sit under mango trees with *better elevenths*
The land is rich and fertile, but the doc's head pays the rents
Intolerance has become the novel honor and respect
The future's grim as we join the shameless prospect!

SOUTH SUDAN

The kitchen is no longer smoky
So, I can see my friends,
The fog has cleared
So, I can drive to the other
Town and be silly,
The other chief has left,
So, I'm no longer confused,
The cabbie on the street smiled at me,
As he congratulates me,
The other lady frowns at me,
Because she has no idea,
I have no any other heart to hate
Because freedom is here!

A SINGLE TRIBE SINGING LOUD

We've always been happy for we knew we were right
We've always known we've been free in our *heart*
We've been raped and defiled but we're still strong and upright
We've been told of belligerent tribes from the start
Little did we know, we're just a single tribe singing loud,

We've been named after *you* and told to be quiet
We've been tied down and told we *was* relaxed: not quite
We've been told to say it's safety from the other tribes
We've been induced and coerced into mental stripes
Little did we know, we're a single tribe singing loud,

We've always been scared off but told we *was* timid
We've always been arranged as poor and blinded
We've always been the ubiquitous soul to solace
We've always been the industrious hand of the populace
Little did we know, we're a single tribe singing loud,

We've fought for so long to be liberated
We've fought for so long…even separated
We've fought for so long…even when divided
We've been proselytized to be angry and flabbergasted
Little did we know, we're a single tribe singing loud,

We've been told that that man was a wicked Bari, liar!
We've been told that that woman was a greedy Dinka, liar!
We've been told that that girl is a violent Murle, liar!
We've been told that that boy is a good-for-nothing Nuer, liar!
We've been told that that child is a cowardly Mundari, liar!
Little did we know, we're just a single tribe singing loud,

As the *lies* end, South Sudan is independent
Because we're just a single tribe singing loud!

DESPOTIC LABYRINTHINE: THE WORD

Beyond the valleys of goodness, I naively trod.
Underneath trees of emptiness I wrote
Big verses, long, endearing and winding sentences.
The word oiled me with infantile jolliness.
But the jolly fellows wore weird senses,
The senses that gave me away like a schmuck
The mango fruit I held in hand didn't make me smart.
So, they laughed at me in turns, one covered mouth,
I didn't have to profess my mind, I'm from the south,
But the lingering clouds are gathering rain,
I've worshipped a phantom called goodness in vain,
The valley I tried to cross suddenly swelled,
The trees I'd comfortably sad under mysteriously felled,
The gentle summer wind will whisper away my naivety,
The goodness constant will not be replaced in surety.

THE BEST MUM YOU ARE!

You fetched water from the natural feat
You cooked with woods, not cookers' *eat*
And you had our stomachs smile amidst scarcity
The wild fears you, you're a desire-heart necessity
Happy mothers' day, for you're the best.

You cooked for all even the mouths you didn't know
You welcome all even the dirty with no time to sow
They smiled away their hunger many times in a row
They praised you for the food but for you saw…
Saw the endearing heart with limitless woe
Happy mothers' day, you're the best.

You smile every sorrow away anytime you think
It's that quality we wanted to ape for all things
We crossed dangerous rivers; our hearts didn't sink
Dad knew the leader he chose for a wife is a mind sublime
In your hand we remain proud and appreciative.

Among all, you're the one and only
Happy mothers' day, mama. We love you!!!

AS THE BLACK STRIPE ASCENDS

O, South Sudan, out of obscurity you've emerged strong
We praise and glorify you, for the martyrs sing your song
Your sons and daughters bled and will still bleed in defence
The land of great warriors, the land of unwavering essence
Oh mighty South Sudan, for eternity we'll stand vigilant!

Oh South Sudan, blessed be your infinite and Biblical beauty!
Rise, shine; we'll raise your flag behind the guiding star surety
We'll sing songs of the hard-won freedom with engendered sighs
We'll stand respectful in peace, liberty and justice for all so high
In blood and belief, we will and shall forever make you elegant.

Bless us oh enduring South Sudan! Let savannah greenness smile
Oh land of warriors, uncountable martyrs, forever, truly shine!
Let's stand up in silence and respect your unmatched fauna;
Saluting millions of martyrs under whose name we'll honour
True blood cemented our national foundation: see your flora
We vow to protect our nation, the Nile, skies, for now and ever.

Oh land of our ancestors, freedom you've always willed is here!
Land of respectable fauna and flora, of industrious seers
Uphold us united in peace and harmony and let guns be in silence
The Nile, valleys, forests, and mountains will be clear of vigilance
Vegetation in peace shall be our perspicuous source of joy and pride.
Let us worship our Gods and hold our faiths in a blessed prize.

Oh South Sudan, you're smiling, you're free and you're strong,
Let the circumambulating voices be forever a joyful throng,
Allow us an enduring chord to yell out forever a very humbling song,
Present a wise leadership to guide the joyous crowd not to be wrong,
Oh South Sudan, we've yearned for years not to be pitiable mongs!

And here at last we are!

TIMES NEVER TRANSCEND

Dreaded piety, what do you want?
Flawed phenomenon, try me;
Delighting on reflective me,
Grassy change is required,
But hear me, it's only
Seven and I know that times
Will never transcend;
Hear me as always.

WHEN HATE MAKES 'YOU' FEEL GOOD!

Death is nobody's friend,
It's a complete certainty at the end,
We are all organically the same,
Even if opinions make life a game.
Tell me what you'll say in the morrow!

Many divisive factors we face,
They become fuels of the love defaced,
We become divisive simpletons
 As we grow as hate-fill automatons,
 But what will you say in the morrow!

Do you believe what you say now?
Vision togetherness and tell me how?
We embrace our own in bitterness
Forgetting that the end game is togetherness,
Tell me what you'll say in the morrow.

If hate makes you feel good and proud,
Then see a future in fire, smoke cloud.
I know 'I don't care' comes easy to you;
'Cause of the loved ones lost in madness spew,
But tell me what you'll say in the morrow!

SMILE LITTLE GIRL!

You'd always wanted to sit under that mango tree
As your dad always prayed for you to be free.

Smile for the land will welcome you to see;
To see that dad was right for your face's glee.

Your dark face comforts the unstable unstable;
Your wire thin trunk speaks of the valor that's noble.

You'd endured bad stare, bad piety: all troubles.
But hey, little girl, Smile, your mango won't wobble.

Smile for you're free; smile for you're redeemed;
Smile for your land will never, again, be condemned.

Pick up that mango and slice it down your throat with a sigh.
Smile little girl for you'll soar with the sudd birds: be high.

Swim the length of the Nile with the friendly crocodiles nearby.
They'd missed your beautiful, crispy chirping no one can buy.

Fly over the tropical rain forest and breathe in your freedom.
Smile little girl for you're free, and dive into stardom.

Smile little girl!

I'M JUST A LIAR

It's not that I'm not a liar,
His end just put me on fire.
It's in my heart to desire,
Only that I'm there to expire.
So much said to be entire,
Words keep flying to my tire,
By the roadside I sat in dire,
The Samaritan blamed me for hire,
You laughed at me when I passed,
For humility has taken me to the past,
It's not that I'm not a liar,
It's the best that I admire.

It's not that I'm not a liar,
The truth was taken for me to expire,
It's not that I'm not lazy,
I'm emptied to see the world hazy,
It's not that I'm not strayed,
Respect isn't in the holiest prayed,
It's not that I'm not mindless,
I write a lot to be penniless,
It's not that I don't care,
Nature took my father just to stare,
It's not that I'm not stupid,
My work got lost by my Cupid.
It's not that I'm not a liar,
It's just because I lost a father...
And that's why I'm a liar!

THE ABSOLUTE

He told off the big men of empiricism,
Behind him was his thoughts' simplism;
His protection's the sharpness of his ego,
But science is not a weak man's feat also,
Even if you think you bath in its glory,
The luxury you think it is isn't the story,
You must toil to be 'scienced' like the antiquities;
The Axial Age is when time spoils indignities,
The test tube is not enough to be science,
For glory of the toil is ripped even in silence,
The moustached fellow was brave,
You told me the luxury would be grave,
The absolute is real
The relative is a reel
Our minds are tested in time
Space-time is to mock the wise past in mime,
That told off the men of antiquities,
Because he's protected by his indignities.

THE SKEPTIC AND DENG PAKENY

This is the Baal's way,
And it is also true like Deng Pakeny,
The Jews had their tribal deities,
But lorded one over us with shameless indignities;
Oh, it was the Yahweh's Europe,
Murderous deity was an indescribable sucker:
Jealous, genocidal, tribal and intolerant,
No wonder the Israelites had no problem
Forgetting him with ease, what Elohim?
They had lewd rituals, but they thought
The obscene was the Southern (Upper) soul,
Their Yahweh was mystical and mythical,
Deng was represented as angry
As Yahweh but not by any means a misogynist,
Yahweh was slick but deluded; changing
His name now and again; getting
Moses, Abraham, Joshua, Isaac and Amos
Confused...today forgiving and tomorrow
Unleashing vengeance. . .anthropomorphic sucker!
Deng Pakeny endures through the real time
And through Einsteinian Kantian space-time,
I have my deities; go with your dying ones.

In Honor of Isaiah Abraham

So the pied pipers believe they've won!
They should've known you were on a mission, son
A mission you respected by all available means:
Gun, Pen, Word, Brain, Will, Guts and Honor
How about the boss and his Chihuahuas?
They were, like us, our camp dwellers
I hear they're very terrible spellers
So for them, Freedom and Prison are the same
Magnifying their ghostly achievements is now a game
But do they know this specialty?
Yes, them…
…that a writer's quiddity is his immortality
The average mind grapples with this cemented morality
The pied pipers fear and envy this reality
They die and die for good; nothing of them remains
But in Kantian space and time you're not only remains
You're an audacity which time and space hate
But killing a writer is an enormous feat
Fools should know that killing thoughts is a risk
They hate you for those impeccable writs
It's the writ that dwarfs the pious eternity
You're in eternity— even fools now write with certainty
But how did you do it, we might ask?
Conscious awareness is now for everyone a task
You've shown the power of reason
Those cows know they're only a season
That thought alone is a red pepper in their eyes
Excuse them; they're traumatized by dollar signs
But you only wanted a land the dear doctor wanted:

A land of free thoughts with no one exempted
A land in which potentials compete
A land in which competition breeds
A land in which brilliance is celebrated
A land in which only prosperity is calibrated
But you didn't sleep in vain
Even when we're left in pain
Your words and thoughts will smile in us
 Smile in us even when the pied pipers rust
How long do they have anyway?
Sleep brother; honor you've sprayed
And never will we be swayed
Cowards can't cow us into cowardice
Go in peace: your pen's ink still flows nice
The eternal word of the writer!

THE VILLAGE GIRL WONDERS

I thought the 'educated' were kind,
Well, I was told to 'never mind,'
The village girl walks around half naked,
Well, her *bra* was her only jacket,
The *educated* sees me and twists her lips,
I smile as she swayed her hips,
I love her colorful outfit;
Only that her attitude makes me spit,
She was so 'educated' I was told...
Educated but never likes books? That doesn't hold!
The village girl dresses based on needs,
And she impresses in choice indeed!
The village girl like the *educated Achol* is kind;
But this educated *face* is a non-spelling kind,
She's from Florida, she said...
But she thought Florida's the capital of the state,
But she wonders why men there like us,
We, the village girls will talk without masks
As the *educated* looks ghostly anytime she passes,
I love America so much
But this *educated* face puts it bad as such,
I am from the village,
But the village is now *redefined.*

WHAT A CHILD YOU ARE!
(In everything, daddy loves you!)

Atet, you're already, indeed, four,
I'm happy like never before,
But I seem like a lousy dad,
You'll soon learn the reason in that.

Distance has been monstrous,
I write everyday a legacy lustrous,
I apologize for not being there,
In time they'll know and stare.

And you'll have history to smile from,
She'll place you snugly on her bosom,
Unique fathers come once in a while,
I had one, so I want you to smile.

You shower me with wits at your age,
I'm not surprised: you're blood of sage,
The sage is not me: your grandpa, the man,
 You tell me off and I smile: a proud man.

You always consider your grandma,
The sweetest thing from a child with no drama,
You're beautiful so needn't I say more,
Thoughts of you are my therapy out of moor.

I write knowing it's all for you,
Even when I seem distant and screwed,
We won't change the world,
But the world will know we had a word.

Happy birthday Atetdit!
Daddy loves you!

A BEAUTIFUL MIND, A BEAUTIFUL VOICE, A BEAUTIFUL HEART

For Nyankol Mathiang, a cultural icon

We were numbed and shocked out of our breaths
But your deeds traveled the nation's breadth
Who dare compare in all vain arrogance?
The simpletons could be excused of their ignorance
Your legacy marathoned with your humanity
Your soulful voice competed with your words' profundity
And the innocent felt your counsel even by hearsay
We wipe our tears away for your words are here to stay
Forever will you be a mother because of whom no going astray
We knew the rain rained on us like divine's freedom
Our disaster preparedness are your words, your counsel, wisdom
The nation assumed the meanings even when all didn't understand
Translation was needless for your heart assumed the right stance
They trusted the mother they'd come to know
Orphans leaned on your words as the world pulled them into sorrow
Widows and widowers had a *friend,* a friend even god couldn't throw
Leaders lied with guilt knowing Mama's wisdom policed, words in tow
You've left us in pain, but left us with profound motherliness: we bow!
The Southern brother knows the uniqueness of the dark sister
Few could've done it with no crispy voice, efficient, sublime transistor
Abroad, you amplified our hopes and regulated our pain
For your word the oppressed endured torture, dungeon, but still sane
Your prophetic mind advised with precise comfort
Togetherness you advised became our salvation port
None other than Garang and Riek attested to your sort
Mama we cry for too soon you've been taken
Mama we cry for we're broken

***

Mama we still laugh for your name will last

61

Even in sorrow and pain you maintained so much class
In you we had a teacher
In you we had a sister
In you we had a mother
In you was a comforter like no other
We could cry for years, but so much you've done to be immortalized
Even the wicked will turn to your words and be moralized
Rest in perfect, impeccable peace
Your job is done. This is your legacy, your *word!*

A FANCY OF COLLEGIALITY

We could as well call those teeth white,
Because that desired collegiality will go after the night
It'll evaporate into political flimsy air, the sun in sight.
Good old sun edges the fogginess just to make things right,
It's not the sun of Grecian mythical Icarus.

We could drain in the words of those righteous old men.
After all their verbatim have become divine: Amen!
Who says the poet has to be polite as to invent?
It's the respect of the narratives in the advent;
Advent of the truth to the quibbling poachers and rhinoceros.

We knew the truth from the inculpatory pulsating.
But 'who cares' will be the mantra from brusque exculpating.
Bitterness veiled in wantingness breeds fantastic erring,
But this is denied in the name of loose collegial bearing.
Ignorant fancy of collegiality is dangerous.

But the 'fancists' invented a phantasmal collegiality.
After all the fancists claim the righteous old men 'originality',
They might be right for collegiality is assumed sublime;
Nominal togetherness born out of rapacious rapine
You'll pardon the poor poet for this field is egregious.

SMILE, IT'S A BEAUTIFUL WRIT

I don't hate banana and coconut milk,
My body only stiffens like silk
When that poison, for my work, is the aid.
It's the only need I never said,
Please, on the table, put an amiable glass.
I've gained and lost all with no class.
The body is blighted by mignon voices.
Poetry, thoughts, the despicable choices,
But smile...it's a beautiful writ!

Dreams aren't fantastic,
Phantasmal mewls aren't realistic
But behind the desk with a pipe and a cup
Is the writing lad with a banal thought.
The whining throng frowning 'ought'.
It's the emptiness they've sung for eons.
The words sharpened and arranged like neon,
They shine the way that's despised for grits.
But smile...it's such a beautiful writ!

We've seen words arranged like beads;
Shining, shaming the throngs as he reads,
The pain is monstrously sharp
The songs of the sung penmanship stab
Like the coconut milk on him; he's seen thus.
Poor lad writes damning thoughts on the bus,
Who cares what this lad brings,
The loser sings,
But no, he says, smile; it's such a beautiful writ!
Mango juice under a mango tree shade
Makes the lad feel wow under a beautiful glade;

But when did you become this?
Banana that makes him diseased!
His beautiful words are tormenting.
His beautiful face is just pretending.
The pen is bleeding; the mind perspiring,
The eyes red, 12 hours behind white screens.
The future he sees in greens,
All tired of eons past, but smile indeed
What a beautiful writ?

HEARTLESSNESS THAT'S SO KIND

For the goodness inside us all

I've always quarrelled with the lonely trees
Yeah, madness only comes in degrees
I respect all but what's madness worth?
How did your heart turn into stone?
But oh, it's something you'll figure alone
You can take me for what you are
We're all kind if you look from a far
I'm a sad man because I've chosen to
Some flashes of happiness I've been through
I write so I have to be the dumbest rationalist
Humility will make me a sound nationalist
But hold on…. there's heartlessness that's so kind
You can take my hand and you'll see me smile
I'm a box layered up not just for a while
My hidden me will shock you in style
See yourself in me but know I'm a breed
South Sudanese in and out for all my deeds
You can doubt that but it's so true
You claim to be good. It isn't yet untrue
You claim to be kind, the heavens now squirm
Deep in you is the saddest nymph to confirm
I'm a sad man because I've opened my eyes
I'm a kind man because I let things pass by
But hold on…there's heartlessness that's so kind
You can take me for what you think
Then at night you cry looking into the sink
I don't blame you. That's humaneness in you
You can't hide it…it breathes in kindness too
I don't know how kindness could be so…
But hold on…the world always knows

I'm a sad man because kindness my heart owes
You can shred me to pieces but remember the truth
I hate truth because it's so arresting and blue
The Africanness in me is the goodness you see
I'm a bad man so I'll just let you be
But hold on...I know you're hurting inside
There's softness of heart I can see beside
I'm a sad man because I've chosen peace
I'm a weak man sick of truth disease
I ask myself how kindness could be so heartless
You can take me for what you are
But I still wonder…..
I love the kindness of humanity
I hope you'll one day smoke humility
But hold on...I'm still wondering of…..
The Heartlessness that's so Kind

IN PEACE YOU WILL REST!

Your words were few but meaningful,
Your deeds were small but agreeable,
Death ends a good life,
But fool it is for it ends not a good mind.
Respect isn't forced but earned,
And mine you took to the grave in hand.
Many words aren't required,
For you wasted not your life aside,
Dad glorified your house,
And nothing else for my mind also does,
So much pain do I remain with,
But your children will I delight in,
Not so much will I promise,
But peace and love will you go with.
Rest in Peace Cousin.
Woe death, the assassin.

JUST IMAGINE

Imagine forgiveness without accountability
Imagine relations with no due sensitivity
Imagine mockery on your face with no humaneness
Imagine scorns invited then denied in oneness
Imagine morose loads served with a smile
Just imagine!

Imagine life full of laughter but no respect
Imagine love to drive life with no prospect
Imagine weird dreams dreamed in a clueless tribe
Imagine words spoken in an unorthodox stripe
Imagine a land making creativity senile
Just imagine!

Imagine assumed genius forced with an amazing awe
Imagine animosity, inferiority, hate lined up like death in tow
Imagine a land where difference is a felonious shame
Imagine an education producing idle, foul-mouthed name
Imagine leadership that follows, not lead, along the Nile
Just imagine!

THE REAL AFRICAN MOTHER

She'd weeded the nearly ripe sorghum
The cattle waited for her skillful fingers
She'd always been the graceful mother;
Wearing only a skirt-like piece on her lower self.
The cinnamon skin glowed in the morning rays,
How I loved her ancestral grace!
Her empty breasts flapped on her chest
They've made many warriors and martyrs
She'd told her female seeds the word
The heads they should keep up in elegance
Surprised they didn't remain home,
The mother's tormentors sent them away.
Now her seeds wear funny furs like huts,
She foraged to clothe herself from animals
Now the seeds do so from real humans
She cries for her no-sense-of self seeds
Her seeds have swarmed alien lands
Praise goes to the wind and claimed away
They stare at the mirror and curse
Their skins, now ghostly, leopard-like and winkled.
In foreign neon lights the seeds walk for fortune.
They giggle their penitence away.
'I don't care' has entered into their lexicon;
Mere disguise not what the mother was.

PAMPERING

The angered hearts are a throng
Ever seen angered S'danese with a sarong?
Angered 'cause his wife wore a thong!
Folks see the poet's dark, felonious face
They read into their phony race
The poet covered by a beckoning frondescence
His vain trial smells of indecency.
Calculus on the table
Hawkings on the cable
Still reading naive Dawkins' sample
Musing himself and rapping like a fable
(Yo, is this Nigger word crazy?)
Folks brushed him off. A dear visitor's fart!
The poet's word hurt. Not an open mart.
The fate of Socrates
The undesired nemesis
Who cares anyway?
Stupid for wasting his words away
Does he think really?
Ignorant insouciant rally
Of course, they understand.
It's only the pampering they stand.

NATO

Thursday, October 20, 2011
Notoriously Atrocious,
Self-righteous,
But a
Totalitarian Oligarchy.
Encore:
Notoriously Atrocious
Totalitarian Oligarchy...
I present to you...
NATO.

DEATH OF INTELLECT

When wonders end
Will we be sane?
When tragedy strikes
Opportunism spikes
I have reasons to be awed and teary-eyed
We've self-stupefied eating our French fries
Men have scaled off their good essence
Vengeance has become good pretense
The wisdom of yesteryears is crucified
'I don't care!' has birthed a load satisfied
Hidden imbecility is hiding no more
Ancestral goodness now of useless mores
Self-sacrifice has become a Facebook dare
Young, *educated* warriors fooled to stare
Tragedies *celebrated* in reptiles' orbs
Allegiance dreads the dirty switch
Tomorrow concerns are left for the witch
Who cares about it anyway?
Death of intellect all the way
Interest has transcended integrity
Jealousy has become the celebrity
Ask me why I shouldn't weep
Jonglei has become the fools' arena
Unity is obliterated as if the panacea
Upper Nile is a jittery leverage
Tell me where intellect lives on average?
Who cares about intellect when death floats?
Who cares about integrity when interest stops?
The wise have become the don't-care fools
The tragic result of years spent in school
Will it only be an imbecility hangover?

73

What a quick and sad turnover?
Death of the mother and child is tragic
Death of grandma and grandpa makes us sick
And death of intellect is a disaster in the making
Death of intellect is ready to destroy...
South Sudan... the tragedy...the fools play toy!

WE ARE STILL IN A DUNGEON, DOC

For John Garang & the martyrs

Would you be surprised that we are still crying?
Would you be surprised that we are still dying?
With CPA we thought we'd had eternal salvation
Now, Brothers and Sisters focus energies into self-destruction
The wail of the widowed mother would make you weep
The homelessness of the orphaned is sadness so deep
SPLM & SPLA have been converted into a slaughter-house
The noble twins are no longer our salvation brass
Elders 'eat' our resources with a shameless grin
Years when elders cared are gone, never to be seen
You started at the precipice only to unite the populace
Thousands sought comfort in what became a noble race
So, Dr. John, we're still in a sadness dungeon
We cried when you passed but then you'd done your job
We wiped our tears knowing we could no longer be robbed
You brought us CPA with a flamboyant fail-safe button
Kiir did his best for the South not to be forgotten
But the task you left has proven to be an enormous feat
He's buried from head to toe in a bottomless pit
And into that pit South Sudan is falling in
South Sudan's beauty is razed down by brothers within
Your colleagues copied Khartoum with a photo precision
Your colleagues have become jobbists in every decision
Now it's Juba that's 'too deformed to be reformed'
South Sudan is now just free on paper
Only fools would be happy with eyes rubbed in pepper
You've not died in vain but life ain't easy either
We've been tested and divided but we'll go farther
Struggle became our name since the first slave raid

Struggle became our name since the *North* was made
We're still in a dungeon but little girls will be educated
We're still in a dungeon but little boys we'll not be separated
It's hard but it'll always be one nation under the sun
A nation bought with blood of daughters and sons
Ubiquitous drunks dread the word *togetherness*
As if there'll ever be a different nation out in fairness
We're in a dungeon but we'll never ever give up
No one knew a nation called South Sudan would rise up
Nyuon Bääny and Arok Thon wouldn't want us bleeding
Kuanyin Bol would hate Juba pot-bellied, now stealing
The martyrs have not died in vain, but mothers' lives are hard
We're still in a dungeon but you'll always be in our hearts
You wanted to make us dignified owners and you did
Now, we ask that guns be silent for us to just be!
We're still in a dungeon but we'll always be & see!

WE MISS YOU LIKE NO WORK CAN DESCRIBE

It's been eight years, but it feels like yesterday
With every passing day you're missed
With every reason to say, you're still vivid
Too many reasons to want you here
The metaphysical realities are non-issue
The affective implications are thrown our way
It's emptiness not fillable under this solar flare
The other day they told me a reason
To think about you, the silence made the world...
Big, wicked and presumptuously chiding
The other day they told me words to realize
They aren't you and will never be
YOU are one reality they'll never replace
I have reasons to cry loud
I have reasons to be reserved and be
Shouted at by the throng, which wants
The unwanted done
I have reasons to despise when I call
And nothing happens
I have reasons to be lonely in a sea
Of confused multitude that only sees
A nerd...always reading, writing and singing
The unfathomable *me* has reasons to despise
I have reasons not to have things done;
Not that they want anything done anyway
I have every reason to be a whiner,
For nature left me a lone...the wall
I thought existed behind was only
A figment of my thoughts...
A lot can't be done...
Because they didn't want you here.

Rest in Peace Dad!

CHASING DREAMS

They come to the world with vivid dreams
Drummed into them by the glamorous gleams.
It's the truth they have to face...
If not the dead of everyday race,
Water and wine is all too the same,
The indulgence, the praise that becomes a game.
Their talents so much an intoxication thrust into the world,
Overwhelming it becomes too much to say the word.
The talent the world yearns for is there too much...
We'll now appreciate the ignored mind as such.
Gone too soon are they.
This is a loss you can never have too much to say.
RIP! Rest in deeds!

She always hoisted that red satchel over her right shoulder any time she saw his short steps, lousy gaits and smashingly milky smile.
It was always several seconds to minutes before she realized the reflex.

She loved books; he hated them; he loved to run; she hated that...so said the teacher. What deity should she pray to? What deity was that cruel?
But still she fancied the feeling and the power of true attraction, even under the cold of the biting winter, the *thought* of him warmed her, head to toe.

She'd braced for the worst, both in her integrity and the truism in her emotions. Books meant so much to her...am I not getting insane? But true attraction can't be misinterpreted. As she opened the locker, she heard a *pow* of his flip flops.

Over her left shoulder, she could see him stealing a meaningful and endearing glance at her. "Stop dreaming, he's too good, but stupid for you!" She's always been a good mentor to her own *self*...not when she saw him though.

True love never lies...as she closed the locker, he was standing shyly behind her. She was lost for words, so he said: "I see you like math. I love it too; can we study together?"

.

REAL WOMAN, SOUTHERN WOMAN

On her face is a smile
But vanity she hates
With beauty in her mind
No skin she envies
Hard-work she knows
But gothika's no gates
A well-kept and desired soul
A real woman with a mind lives
Reads
Reflects
Decides.

She loves real men
Not the talking type
She stands elegant
Her pallid friend saw no wig
Her voice is loud not only then
Wig?
Her face is desired, ever nice
Ever ...

THE PLEBISCITE IS HERE!!

Vote with your all

You've dreamed, waited earnestly for darn long
It's now your time to simmer, shine and belong
Years had withered you in that 'pious' throng
You still stood with unmatched valor and strong,

They've laughed, amused at your very desires
Because your tired and humble soul always cries
Don't cry but point the finger that always implies;
Implies your hope, clad in colorfulness, now flies

The doctor said: *you'll never be the same again*
What he'd said in forceful essence is your gain;
The gain of your toils as you wait for next rain
You'll joyously let the happy water into the drain,

The mango tree shade awaits your celebration
The lemon tree dreams of lemonade in attention
The crocodile flosses her teeth at what you'll ration
She's happy for your friendship is an exception,

I'll stop there for I'm ecstatic and full of tears
It's a burden of joy that no true man truly bears
But I'll watch you cast your ballot which clears;
Clears away the doubt as we wait with lots of beers.

DEAR SANTA: THE WRITER'S WISH!

Simple

I'd like Jacksee to twist them
Poetic words so that I laugh
Till my ... my. . .never mind!
Dekuek will poetically inform
My naïve political mind. . .
So, I'm like, how old is he again?
Tearz writes and I tearfully
Understand the rapacious generals,
Thieves, I mean, Chiefs. . .
Then Apuk will make my mind
See vividly: Oh, the poetic genius;
She makes my mind see!
Then Penn will frog-match
The Black Christs with poetic-leaks:
They are still writing, Boo! Security fellow!
Then Nyadol will tell my sisters
To be strong and informed,
So, Sabbath writes a romantic
Poem to our princesses:
Now they kiss under
The mistletoe! Ha ha!
And when I see Eunice write:
Happiness!
I say, 'hey, stupid fat man. . .
Respect my earth's mother:
The Queen of the Nile!'
So now, let her rock the runway,
Ms Gatbel, that is!
Oh, that simple!

But that is my wish!
Happy Holidays!

PROSAIC THOUGHTS

She heralds the end of hominid breath
Brilliance that makes *smart* out of fools
You can't wonder why big men shiver when she passes
Enduring lessons you can't get in school
She's assumed a witch but she's the equalizing best
The best moralist with the granny stool
All thoughts give way: 'her boat harasses!'
No, she's *the* towering truth ending 'us' in a spool
Too much timidity...which is all too prosaic
Wonder why she makes us fearful maniacs?
Perhaps only the twisted fanatics know her best.

THAT LITTLE GIRL OVER THERE

I was reading 'A Brief History of Time'
So you twist your lips in that hiemal clime
You wonder what a dunce I could be
You could have hurled bitter words at me
But because of that little girl over there.

She amazed me: just at ten-years old
You'd showed your yellow teeth I was told
Yeah, that embarrassing mouth you hate to show
I wonder why cover it if you don't want it so
I guess it's because of that little girl over there.

I'd told her amazing things I'd planned
She'd whispered the bitterness you'd earned
No wonder you've lost so much weight
I'd smiled when she told me your wait
You could've sneered, but that little girl over there?

She's so amazing you know
Not that you give any rat's ass: yeah, manners I grow
But mind not because I pull an all-nighter
It's the same plan she'd told you, just being nicer
You could've pulled the plugs of my plans
But remember, that little girl over there!

THE BURDEN OF VIRTUE

For you I smile!

Then

I saw the orange sun go down!
I slept knowing I was good
Little did I know I was a fool,
Long did I stay in school;
Only to know the burden of virtue!
I saw all in the grass at dawn
I saw something called *smile*
Then it disappeared, me senile,
All because I was true;
Stupid me: the burden of virtue!

Now

I watch the orange sun-set
Knowing that I'm reset
You took my hand in earnest
And kissed it so nice and dearest
I now know what it means to smile
When you say, 'me too' in a while
We've laughed as if we were born the same…
There's something in you I can't name
It hit me like a truck
Fools say time is of essence, oh schmucks!
Take my heart and keep it like a glass
You left me with so much class
Good memories I'll cherish
Unpretentious heart, your love never will perish
It's the tenderness I remember,
And the sweet excuses to just see me smile!

With lady grits and wits, you told me
The burden of virtue!
Your unpretentiousness I'll see again!

BELL OF THE SOUL

I'd forgotten the color of my teeth,
For eons I've been bottled up indeed
And there you are, like a caring puppy,
You squeezed that laugh out of me-duddy,
And man is there a reason to smile,
A beautiful heart, beautiful mind, you're the style,
Belle of the soul, that's all I say!

Your face mocks what blighted me
I've subitize happiness for all to see
Now, cunctation and sorrow you've blown
Your mignon authenticity is all but shown
Thrown and blown but sweet kindness you are
Venus in my sky, first and the only star
No longer a fantast so, belle, that's all I say!

You whispered those mignon words
You arrived from an unpretentious world
The cracked glass is there so apparent
Passionate miracle, you performed the errant
It all sounds bosh, but man, are you special
Authentic face, authentic skin, so gentle.
Ravelment is past, so, belle, that's all I say!

STUPID ME

I wanted to lie, but stupid science
I wanted to be lazy, but crazy technology
I wanted to say the truth – religion says no
I wanted to be fair, but capitalism's wicked
I wanted to work hard, but communism says others
South Sudanese only, so Jesus the Jewish boy cried
Deng Pakeny, Aleer and Mayom wondered:
"God?" Christianity?
"Isn't this dude the Jewish *jok*?"
He capitalized his name Yahweh, 'God'
What an arrogant racist!
I wanted to laugh, but the dentist took it
I thought I worked hard... but god said he did it for me
He makes self-esteem hard...stupid old man
I thought death was like sleeping:
Stupid pious talk of hot hell
I wanted to go to church, but they ask me money
I wanted to pray... but god seems stubborn
He knows what I want, but wants me to say it anyway
He watches over us, but pretends he doesn't
Stupid me!

MOTHER WILL ALWAYS BE THERE

I imagine the pain of labour
I imagine my cries all night long
I imagine the crab I placed all over
Despite all these, you smiled at me
Even as you cleaned while still sleepy
It was for me you didn't sleep
No thanks can ever be enough!

You said don't step out of the house
You told me not to see that girl
You told me to fetch you a drink
I frowned and said, 'whatever mom!'
Now I imagine if you'd said so at labor.

To everyone, I'm a useless junk
To you, I'm just your baby face jewel
To my friends, I'm unreliable
To you, I'm on the way to reliable
To my friends, I'm arrogant
You smile at me to say the truth
However wretched I become
Mom will always be there!
Love you mom!
Happy Mother's Day!

THE OTHER SIDE OF NO!

That case has never been unambitious
He should have known that skinny malice
The eternal wait was even precious
Humility waited only to police...
This is when they said the other side of NO!

New year ushered in a callous feel
His Lugubrious 'mentals' welcome the deal
The unrequired mind scares the assuming
Under a mango tree his writing desk isn't presuming
And that's why they said the other side of NO!

ABYEI, YOU WILL COME BACK HOME

Déjà vu! Nothing but broken bones and broken promises
Bad, grotesque and impious men in dangerous disguises

∗∗∗∗

Years ago, you were misled into a pretentious consolation
For years you've yearned without confrontation
Coming home has become torturous and intergenerational
You've cried rivers, but solution expected national
You've hemorrhaged plenty, but the world is indifferent
Big men have intervened only to fall back in severance
We watched your homelessness with awful anger
Blackness, charred huts, dead youngsters... a dreadful answer
But what has become of consciousness carers?
What has become of your leaders, who've become starers?
Late Nyankol asked relevant questions only to go unanswered
You've done much for yourself to be free and pampered
But no, your freedom has become bigger than your very being
Promises of 1972 are over and again being seen
You ask yourself what you've done to deserve this
And we ask ourselves how the sleepy leadership persists
The greedy old fellows sold you and passed
But like a strong, sleepy lioness, you won't be suppressed
With white turban and gown comes the impious schemer
With blue suit and tie comes your leader, the clueless dreamer
With tears, blood, death, hunger, wretchedness you remain
We've seen the fat, pot-bellied dreamer in the main
You've been sacrificed as the turban and the tie bargain
You've been abandoned but the dreamers complain
Little to nothing is promised as 2005 promises are now 1972
You've taken it with grace and you'll pull through
Wipe your tears for you need your strength and will

Document your sorrows for you'll need them still
The world saw the smoke of your burning villages
It saw you burn down, watching emotionlessly like savages
Something reminiscent of the savage slave masters
It's difficult to know who's to blame in all quarters
But one thing we all know: your innocence shines
And in the thick of it all we are ashamed, and you'll be fine
All you're asking for is to go home and be free
It isn't too much to ask but it's now at an exorbitant fee
Abyei, you'll come back home!
Funny and sad because you're home but not home
You're near but you're still far
In the end, you'll be a free star!
Abyei, you'll come back home!

TWÏ COUNTY BLEEDS

For the victims of Ajuong and Pakeer massacre

I ain't religious so I cannot pray
You're good so you've become the prey
Hear the broken Twï County women wail
Feel the lost lives of Twï County, away they sail
The garden ploughed with remarkable seeds
These seeds are being discarded in bloody deeds
Who cares when the powerful exalt drunkenness?
Who has the decency to own this shamefulness?
Hear the cry of abandoned Twï Child
Be humane and feel the barefoot kid in the wild
South Sudan is a dishevel and a broken land
Jonglei is barren, a severed hand
Twï County is flooded by blood and grave sands
Ajuong has no tears left to cry
Pakeer has bled its vein dry
Death, Madness and Incompetence
Fear, Complacency and Indifference
The war has ended with more death and destitution
Peace means poverty and political prostitution
We've remained with heavy hearts
This, we didn't know from the start
Blood has flowed for the cause unknown
Murderous adventure and savagery sown
Yet the silence of presidency rings loud
The liars have become objects to be proud
Education has become a quest for stupidity
It amazes us with amazing rapidity
You'll rest in peace knowing you are loved
Rest assured souls that remain will laugh

95

The blood of the dead will wash the land clean
Too much misery we've seen
I guess that's enough to hear the *Twï Child Cry*
South Sudan…you've seen the *Twï Child Bleed*

THE IRRATIONALITY OF DEATH

For Christopher Hitchens

Our third ball is full of felonious douche bags;
Self-righteous throngs circling as reason's snags.
They'd called you wicked.
They'd dreaded you in their old thickets.
Of course, they've never seen him.
They still glorify that adulterous sin.
You showed the dignity of reason,
The existential requirement every season.
The felonious douche bags live long.
They praise their adulterous old man to belong;
To belong when their minds aren't strong.
You wrote the indigestible to the pious,
It's the truth they deny but of their desires.
The end for you will never be in vain,
The universal fate wasn't so much a pain,
It's the elegance you carried to the grave,
It's your bohemian pen that made you brave,
A great mind whose enough cannot be said.
In your friend's word, you stood against all tyranny.
Even god,
Is it not?
Rest my friend, you blessed the world with many!
Death, a friend who knows not any friend.
Knowing the value of your pen,
Too soon it has asked for your name!
What an irrational jerk?

A FAT MAN GOSSIPING, A LEAN GIRL CRYING

By the window, lay a purple vase with a pink flower,
Dear fat John thought it was a mark of his staunch follower,
The fat gossiper whispered a deadly word to Rebecca,
Jeez, John, be a man!
See he just needed a fan!
The mistake was already done as he stood by the baker
He bit the cake and denied it staring at the unbelieving beauty
He's educated but he kowtows to his seasoned friend in reality
His red tie nearly made dear Becky puke,
And dare we say anything for him to refuse
His southside made Nyakong faint
He still brags for the left cake like a saint
Ms. Achol laughed at the *degree* wielded
Fat John has itchy mouth even when shielded
Dear Nyakong suffocated as fat John laughed
And Ms. Achol saw fat Albert at the door; tough!
Where are men of yester *years?*
This is what Nyakong and Achol fear.

A FOOL BLOWN NORTHWARDS BY IGNORANCE

He's groomed for the obvious
Over there and here, he looks civil and serious
Yet he treads on shame, very dangerous!
History calls him to be courageous
Yet, he bows innocently for status
Here he comes: what's his name again?
He's sucked into that loaded game
Only to think that he's being inclusive
They laugh behind his back; very decisive
What a fool?
Oh, he went to school?
And soon he'll be a fool
He's mother called him John
His neighbor laughed a few days later, Hun!
My name is Fun
And so are you: Fun.
And Fun John became
And now the fool is a smart insane
And here comes the inclusive John...
No, I mean Fun.
A cool fool from the south
History-ignorant because of his mouth.
Blame him not: A Bull with a tie!

LOVED IS WHAT YOU ARE

Get well soon, Nyabentiu
Challenge is a word for the strong
Defeat is what's actually wrong
You're strong to dazzle the throng
Loved is what you are
And better you'll be soon
You've given us Precious
Precious she remains and gracious
Our love for you in our hearts is delicious
Loved is what you are
And healthy will you be soon
We're proud of you, beautiful
You achieved the desired and truthful
That stint is nothing for you're dutiful
Smile for loved is what you are
And remarkable you'll get soon
We love you...get well SOON
Nyabentiu!

LOVED YOU WILL ALWAYS BE

I wake up everyday knowing you're smiling
Smile that keeps your old man giggling
You've opened up a world I never knew
It's a thought that makes me always new
And I love you like you'll never know,
Stars are not born but you're my born star
You've washed away life's gruesome scar
Everyday struggles become too small to tell
You're one giant reason for sadness on a scale
And I love you too many times in a row,
Many things are never known in sweetness
Too many minds doubt to key in the sadness
It's the shame you've come to clean
And clean you've done it to gleam
And I love you...and for it, you I saw!
I can now write a verse to dad knowing you
I know what it feels like to be inspired and true
Being a dad is an honor beyond any dreadfulness
The liars of traditional unity are simplemindedness
And I love you from dusk till the rooster's crow
Love you've brought
Love you dispense
Loved you make me feel
And loved you'll always be
Happy third birthday Atetdit.
Dad always love you!!!

TƐT DE WEŊ

It was dark, so I couldn't see
She mooed for my comfort to be
Comforted was I as it rained
Elephants and giraffe, it pained
My wild imagination worked
Ajɔ̈ ë weŋ it must be among ɣɔk
Then came morning with my chagrin
True colors as the sun grins
Tɛt de weŋ acol!
True colors come day light.

RAP, MIC AND THE WORD

The other indigent psyche fears
And so, comes the pious in tears
He's well informed not to be honest
So much is stolen to accept the onus
The rationality train has left
Still believes he's on and the best
I'm afraid of such open piety
It's not me to spoil but the society
His ancestors knew no such son
But dead did he become under the sun
Now he's confused for the word
So, he grabs the mic for the world
He hesitates for his pious spirit
The piety that told him the rare sit
Still, the pious word lingers...
The rap's word angers
The best song comes
It's stupid, the pious sums.

BLISSFUL FRENZY YOU INSPIRE

You are, for all humility and comfort, special
For all eons I'll see that brightly initialed
Time annoys and pleases. . .and runs really fast
But little does time know what you have:
For me you're special and to the world you will be. . .

When the world laughs at me, I know you smile
The joy you give me is never just for a while
It's an eternal bliss that, in hard times, gets me by
I don't do much, but the feeling is too much to deny
You don't do anything to be, for you are and will be. . .

Being yo' dad is a high the Rastafarians'd envy
Every keyboard stroke is a letter in blissful frenzy
You are an angelic mascot even to the impious me
The inexplicable sounds weird but all will see
For now, you are, and tomorrow still, you will be

I'll toil for you to sit like a monarch, but humble
The world will know you're special, but accepting
You're great in being but in life you'll be simple
This is not for you to look back and be bragging
It's for the humility you'll be
Happy fifth birthday, Atedit!

THE PEARL OF THE TORMENTED GIRL

Wow! What an elegant ball of serious prop
Her smile makes our name, our best crop
She has the beauty of the girl next door:
Medium, dark, reserved but likes to shop
She doesn't smile much so that's much in store
Misunderstood and categorized so let's stop
Well, she's mean; that's what we're all for
Yet her beauty trumps our silly thoughts
Sweetness of the girl next door…on the spot
Forbidden love of the clever eye-sore
But let's see who the girl is, underneath
Is she proud or is she tormented in her speech?
Does her beauty hide the demons we can't see?
We've judged her; perhaps we're in for defeat!
The gait and elegance hide a whimpering feat
Her glaring beauty denies her true self
She doesn't want that but we're all deaf
She makes us proud. What about her own *self*?
Too much we pay for the out-ward fresh
Too much we pay for the sweetness we see
Too little we pay for what she'd really be
We've been told to see what pleases, so bleak!
Our eyes subordinate our minds so to speak
We can't see the girl, we see ourselves in her
We can't appreciate her for all we want is there
We can't see her pain because of what *we* want
On billboards she smiles, but beneath she's torn
What a charming smile, what a poisonous herb!
At night her naked body stays rough
Ridges and sliced-up skin we can't know
We can't know because we're beings who only saw

We bow to what we are told to see
If only we could open our minds for her to be
Because that's all she wants, that easy!
She wants the self she knows
A grim negation of what we truly saw
Let's see the tormented girl in real awe
Because that's what she wants, her internal pearl!

FOR YOU, I WILL BE FOR A WHILE

Like Sappho and Hypatia you'll glitter
Around and in your mind, a world cleaner
You're already six and that makes me smile
Like the River Nile, majestic and in style
I'm perhaps a careless father who isn't there
But you know why, and tomorrow is here
I'm sorry I can't pick you up from school
And that silences me and tearful like a fool
But I know you're in good hands
I know a future for you like the Caribbean sand
I know words don't mean much these days
But I know what you said yesterday
Like the loneliest kid on the street
I no longer smile in a world so bleak
But you're my existential sweet
Nothing makes sense if not for you
I can't be there when you cut the cake
And that brings tears that give me no break
You're not just my daughter you're Atet
You're a beautiful gene that's humble
You'll live a remarkable life that's simple
My breeze on a hot summer afternoon
And I smile with you, my hope spoon
I am a father who is never there
But you'll tell the world why I'm here!
I'll see you soon!
Happy birthday Atetdit!

BEREAVEMENT

Loved ones can never, ever be replaced
In your hearts is always their place
Delight in what they meant to you
Exalt their image in what you're going through
Life is a short but a bumpy road
Death is a phenomenon that's broad
It's a thief that defies the highest of securities
We share it with the greatest of all purities
Life is a troubling one-way street
But thoughts of loved ones endure and sweet
Think of them in the nicest way
Seek comfort in the moment of sway
That memorable moment they made U smile
Cherish it always not just for a while
That very single sweet moment is all you need!
For loved ones, all we need is a word to believe!
Forever in our hearts they live!

MY PERFECT STRANGER

I'm a war widow, a single mum with four kids;
'Kids, who'd soon be aimlessly on the streets,'
My pessimistic inner voice mocked,
But *a phone call* stirred me up like a knock,
In life, I've never known good strangers,
Coming from a land of many hidden dangers,
Trust and love were only meant for loved ones
Until I met this perfect stranger, like none!
War and diseases had closed me up…
God, she drained off foreboding in me,
Goodness… I stopped to think trying to see;
Trying to see what the stranger wanted,
Fearful like an antelope being hunted
I screened the genuineness of her smile,
I'm sorry I've left my sense of trust far in the wild
But she shook my hand, firm and reassuring,
She let me in with an attitude that's unassuming,
There and then I knew she's my perfect stranger.
I've always been a refugee, stateless,
But her face said 'no, you are priceless!'
Smiling at me as she closed the door;
A beautiful smile and I nearly fell onto the floor,
Everything she said sounded dreamy,
Weeks later her voice echoed, and creamy,
In school teachers became my kids' strength,
I no longer run from police, very strange!
I'm now not just a woman but a person,
My life no longer feels like a prison,
Canada became a land of helpful 'smilers'
My trauma is no longer a 'spoiler,'
Thanks be to that perfect stranger!

I was blind, but she made me see,
I was hidden but she let me be,
I was lost but she straightened my path,
Simple information put my mind at rest,
Simple information eased my fears,
Simple information gave my kids good peers,
I didn't know teachers could be dear and near,
'Don't smile too much,' another stranger told me,
But, no, I'll keep on smiling...
As long as I have...My PERFECT STRANGER!

BECAUSE I CARE!

For Father Lacombe Nursing Home

'Smile! Smile!' I heard the wind sing
'Take a sigh,' old man winter blinked
My heart was warmed as I entered
My soul was touched and unfettered
For the smile you have, I'll always care
For the beauty of your heart, I'll always be there
Your kindness has essentially brought me here
Holidays are times to give, love and share
Thanks for embracing me with beautiful stares
My soul is here made beautiful
Your open heart has made me wonderful
Your love is the blessing I seek
The wisdom you have is all I beseech
Let's play together!
Let's dance together!
For you, there's me
For me, there's you, you see?
Heaven blesses us with a purpose
Care is all we need to prosper
Smile! Smile! It's the soul's food
Dance! Dance! It's happiness so good
Tell me you'll be happy and free
You're here and your wisdom I see
Your smile brightens my day
Your wisdom I'll cherish everyday
You've made the world a better place
That's why all I see is grace
Smile! Smile! Smile!
Your presence blesses my heart!

Take my humble hand and heart!
I'm here at your service...
Because I care!
And because you care!

THE ANGELS ABOUT!

I see!

They walk on two legs
And trample on hatched eggs;
But then they need chicken,
'Cause they're the Angels about.

They see the poor beg,
They smile eating Indian cake;
They 'care' as the poor sicken!
'Cause they're the Angels about.

They disregard the nation's fate
As the poor eat leaves for steak;
But shrug off the plight stricken,
'Cause they're the Angels about.

I see!

They care amply for the poor
So they allow them to die.
That tininess with a cup by the store,
Isn't drinking tea as she sits by.
She needs two maize grains.

Wire-thin and skeleton-like,
She stares as the Angels are about
With Pajero full of beers!

So I see the Angels about!

THE CANADA I DIDN'T KNOW AND THE CANADA I WANT TO SEE

> It is time for parents to teach young people early on that in diversity there is beauty and there is strength.
>
> **— Maya Angelou**

AS AN AFRICAN MAN, I know monstrous, skewed judgements as the order of my days in Calgary, Alberta. About a month ago, my cousin's wife was called the 'N' word by a lady driving by, saying that 'she should be shot.' This happens more often, but who wants to hear the whining souls? They're isolated incidences, you'd say!

I've been subjected to situations that can, in essence, be traumatizing. However, I've risen above and beyond such denigrating epithets in Canada. I've defined myself in a way that makes it difficult for outside opining and judgements to have a lasting effect on my emotive states.

From speaking English, to the manner I speak, to the clarity of my speeches, to the nuanced philosophical nature of my statements, I'm first placed in a weaker position on a daily judgment scale. However, something else bothers me about others, who are not able to fend away judgements about themselves. Like my cousin's wife! They don't have the means and methods I have, to air out their thoughts and frustrations. That's tragic!

The more immigrants live in Canada, the more their sense of 'alienness' is sown and watered. It's always the case that immigrants feel great attachment to Canada a few years after arriving. However, as years drift by and they start to understand all the operational intricacies, a sense of *the* hidden 'otherness' creeps in gradually.

However, this is not something the mainstream society understands because immigrants tend to hide their disappointments in order to impress their host country: be grateful. This presumed positive impression tends to fade away slowly but consciously and they come to the unfortunate realization that 'you came here from somewhere.'

There is this wedge (that I'm Canadian but ideally foreign) that is planted (unconsciously) by the mainstream. This wedge pulls immigrants away from the core of what makes Canada tick. But the mainstream doesn't always get it because the operations of such aliening attitudes have been exceptionally normalized to a point where their effect is not felt. It clearly takes a conscientious Canadian to pause and take a look at such instances.

Exceptional cases such as immigrants, who have made it to public offices, are masqueraded as examples of what Canada actually is. This is a dangerous fallacy that is a great disservice to immigrants and Canada in the long run. You don't correct what is good, you correct what is bad.

However, these instances (of unease among immigrants) are only heeded if there are stakes to the person who develops an interest in understanding such instances.

Having had the privilege to work with immigrants from different parts of the word, and as a writer and author who doesn't take issues at face value, I've come to realize that Canada needs to do more to make immigrants part and parcel of the Canadian society.

Multiculturalism is a fallacious doctrine that continues to be a monstrous disservice to immigrants. It actually keeps the immigrants away from the 'mainstream' by insulating them in their own ethnic and racial enclaves. The mainstream shrugs off the criticism, saying: "We allowed your cultures and languages to flourish what else do you need from us?"

Just imagine a population suffering in silence, a population that has grave grievances and problems but has no way of airing them? Imagine young people living in communities whose leaders are not taken seriously because of where they come from. Imagine a population that is always wary of systemic and societal judgements? Imagine a population that is racially slurred almost on the daily basis, but the mainstream media and population are giving an impression that everything is almost perfect *up here!*

I've had the privilege of putting my thoughts to paper but how about those who narrate to me their dissatisfaction with Canada but have no way of making it known so that the problem is corrected? How about kids who are judged in schools and written off, but no one is there to help them maintain their individual dignity? How about Canadian police who think every African man is a drug dealer?

The more I live in Canada, the more I come to realize that protection of personal niches, however much one wants to project a civil and inclusive face, betrays the wary soul of the privileged heart.

So, what exactly am I saying? The media is the eye and the mirror of society and it's high time it actually treats every single human element in Canada with some respect. The media doesn't have to wait for problems to investigate. It has to help change Canada in a manner no any world media has ever done.

We have to find out what problems are affecting Canadians of different races and ethnic backgrounds and highlight them in order to find solutions. I have to tell you that immigrants are suffering in silence.

They are assumed to be the ones benefiting from Canadian social systems when they are the ones who've filled Canadian factories and warehouses. They are assumed to be the cause of crime in the Canadian communities when the reasons why some of them are so aren't addressed.

Then the less informed Canadian takes what the media says at face value and makes it the judgement truth.

Despite all the lamentable situations I mentioned above, I'm still proud of some societal elements in Canada; however, the more I study and write about social issues, the more I realize that I'd over-exaggerated the inclusive society Canada actually is. I could be wrong; however, no one has actually proven me wrong. I've known a few mainstream Canadians, who are almost messianic in their daily interactions with immigrants, however, they are powerless and their wish to see an inclusive Canada is seen as their naivety and wishful thinking. Who should be surprised?

It's high time, as Canadians, we look at what is said rather than who says it. In the end, we don't know who is going to take Canada to be the next global heart of social and racial inclusive exemplariness.

IS 'BLACK' REALLY BEAUTIFUL? THE IDENTITY OF THE AF-RICAN PERSON

Most people are other people. Their thoughts are someone else's opinions, their lives a mimicry, their passions a quotation.

— Oscar Wilde

THE STATEMENT 'Black Is Beautiful' is always proudly flaunted by Africans and the people of African descent. This simple sentence has been so much vested with power of pride so much so that the possibility that such a statement could mean something negative and racially counterproductive, is never contemplated.

So, when I ask people questions such as "Is 'Black' Really Beautiful?" the immediate answer I get is 'YES.' However, this statement and its 'yes' answer have always bothered me. I've tried as much as I can to understand the meaning and the idea behind the statement. The more I tried to understand it, to get used to it, the more I realized its repulsive implications and the more I realized that the people who utter the statement don't actually think much about it.

People utter it as a question of conventional conformity and tradition enforced from *without*. Asked what the statement means, these people either don't know the meaning of what they utter, or they scratch their heads, lost and confused.

'Black Is Beautiful?' means nothing if not well explained contextually; and in most cases, it's never explained. It even undermines the same people it's supposed to elevate, racially speaking. This statement, for those fond of it, actually reduces a whole *race* to a mere color devoid of human values. Well, this *color* [black] has been vested with values! This is something I find strange and troubling.

However, those who use the statement would want to convince us that 'Black Is' Beautiful' is meant to convey the fact that the people of African descent, or Africans, are *beautiful*. Or more appropriately, the meaning intended is that the skin pigmentation of Africans and the people of African descent is beautiful. This sounds about right because the assumption here is that 'black' is used as a metaphor, or a symbolism for the African Person. But an identity of people as a symbolism is even more troubling. In a sense, an identity should be plain and ungrudgingly respectful.

I don't have any problem with the 'black symbolism' as long as 'black' is used as a metaphor. However, 'black' is not only used as a metaphor. It's been used to forge a proud identity from the very essence of Africanness. We have the *Black Consciousness Movement* in apartheid South Africa, the *Black Panther*, *Black Entertainment Television* (BET)…ctc.

Even when someone mocks *blackness* as a color in itself (not as applied to people), Africans and the people of African descent feel offended. I don't know when I'm allowed to see a difference between *blackness* of the color black *per se* and *blackness* of the Africans and people of African

119

descent? When people say a *black cat* is a sign of bad luck, Africans and the people of African descent feel offended. I get confused. We are talking about a *black cat* and this cat is literally black not figuratively black. These people don't see blackness only as a figurative description, they've owned blackness and see it as who they are literally.

'Black' now means African and African means Black. So, people have become so lost in the *ontic* of their color that they don't see the difference between who they are and the color that has been used to describe them.

Essentially, 'black' is a description used by others to describe Africans and people of African descent. People have become their color and their color has become them. Black is no longer seen as a figurative, derogatory and childish description. That one can separate 'blackness' and Africanness makes some people wonder.

This wonder results from the loss of internal ingenuity in the African Person. Everything for and about the African Person, comes and is enforced by outsiders. Names and derogatory debasement of the whole humanity of the people have been accepted with a remarkable resignation. The fact that blackness was used as an anti-thetical positioning of the African Person on the opposite side of European-ness has been either forgotten or accepted out of powerlessness. A proud identity, unfortunately, has been forged, by the African Person, out of that damning biblical blackness.

'Whiteness,' which now means European-ness, was an elevation of the European Person while Blackness was a debasement of the African Person. The description itself is not bad for each and every race has a knack for self-elevation. What is bad is an attempt by the African Person to either own blackness or to see Africanness and blackness as one and the same.

Instead of African people saying, 'I am Beautiful' as an elevation of a sense of self and beauty, the African Person is so lost to the point that she praises her description. She prides in her description. And this description is by no means glorious! It's an outside imposition; an imposition that was meant to mock her; to place her in a position that's grotesque and undesired.

So, 'Black Is Beautiful' is an elevation of *a description* of the African Person, not an elevation of the *African Person*. Blackness doesn't capture human traditions, values, cultures, intellectual development and the essence of Africanness. Reducing or equating a whole race of people to a mere color is the worst anyone can do to a human population. However, these mad descriptions were understandable during colonialism, slavery, segregation, apartheid, or now, with radically *Racist* people.

The words African, Sudanese, Senegalese, Jamaican, African-American, Haitian, Bahamian, Trinidadian and so forth, have so much respect attached to them in terms of traditions and human values. They represent, not describe people. These words are full of meaning. I hear Jamaica and my mind goes straight to vibrant people with traditions and values. I hear 'African-Americans' and I see ingenious people with values and traditions. I hear 'Black People' and I'm stuck with emptiness and intellectual loss. To reduce these proud people to a mere *color* is terrible, socially detrimental.

I want people with a respectable import, to see themselves as separate from their describing *color*. When we say, 'Black is Beautiful,' is it the blackness of Barack Obama or blackness of Kuir ë Garang, or that of Soledad O'Brien? We don't look the same color-wise so why should we be described by the same color? What is common among the three of us is not blackness; it's the African *blood* in all of us. To reduce our human connection to a mere *color* is a terrible offence. However, we've become so used to being mocked and described that to question such things sounds like some martial hermeneutic.

So, "Is 'Black' Really Beautiful?" No! But you are beautiful! Never say 'Black is Beautiful!' Just say, 'I am Beautiful!' Beauty is a quality of individuals not a quality of a Race. And beauty should not be sought in descriptions, but in the people *per se*.

Thök de Ka

.